Contents

Differences

We are all different ages and sizes. We all have different coloured hair and skin. We are all good at different things.

Reading

We read words.

We read sentences.

Sometimes we read to learn. Some people need glasses to read.

Sometimes we read for fun.

Sometimes people read to us.

How we read

People read in different ways.

People read in different places.

Some people read from left to right.

Some people read from right to left.

Braille

Some people read with their fingers.

headphones

Some people listen to sounds to help them read words on a screen.

character

Some people read characters.

Some people read letters.

What we read

Sometimes people read books.

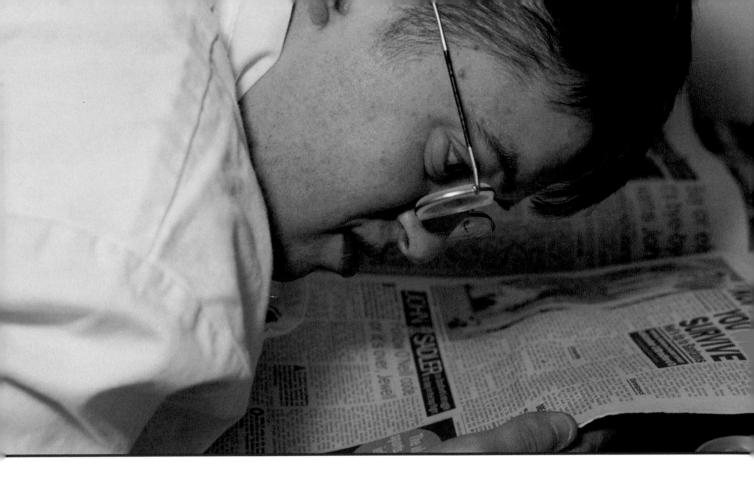

Sometimes people read newspapers.

Sometimes people read signs.

Sometimes people read
using computers.

We are all different

There are lots of different ways to read. How do you read?

Words to know

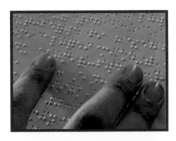

Braille raised bumps on paper.
People read Braille with their fingers.

glasses small pieces of glass worn over
the eyes. Glasses help some people see.

headphones small speakers people
wear over or inside the ears.
Headphones help people hear.

Index

Note to parents and teachers

Before reading

Talk about the ways people are the same and different. Some of the differences are physical or mental, and some are because different people like different things – but all people are special and all people are equally important. Ask the children why they think it is important to learn to read. Point out that we don't only read books: we can read from a whiteboard, a computer, magazines, and words on signs and on television.

After reading

Show the children some examples of Braille, and let them feel the raised dots. Help them make their own "Braille" letters by piercing holes in the shape of letters through thin card. Turn the cards over and see if they can "read" the letters.